S0-BMT-913

What's Awake?

Skunks

Patricia Whitehouse

Heinemann Library
Chicago, Illinois

© 2003 Reed Educational & Professional Publishing
Published by Heinemann Library,
an imprint of Reed Educational & Professional Publishing,
Chicago, Illinois

Customer Service 888-454-2279
Visit our website at www.heinemannlibrary.com

All rights reserved. No part of this publication may be reproduced or transmitted in any form or by any means, electronic or mechanical, including photocopying, recording, taping, or any information storage and retrieval system, without permission in writing from the publisher.

Designed by Sue Emerson, Heinemann Library
Printed and bound in the United States by Lake Book Manufacturing, Inc.

07 06 05 04 03
10 9 8 7 6 5 4 3 2 1

Library of Congress Cataloging-in-Publication Data
Whitehouse, Patricia, 1958-
    Skunks / Patricia Whitehouse.
        p. cm. — (What's awake)
Includes index.
Summary: A basic introduction to skunks, including their habitat, diet, and physical features.
    ISBN: 1-58810-883-X (HC), 1-40340-630-8 (Pbk.)
    1. Skunks—Juvenile literature. [1. Skunks] I. Title.
    QL737.C25 W53 2002
    599.76'8—dc21

2001006397

Acknowledgments
The author and publishers are grateful to the following for permission to reproduce copyright material:
p. 4 Steve Strickland/Visuals Unlimited; p. 5 Tom & Pat Leeson/Photo Researchers, Inc.; p. 6 Jeff Lepore/Photo Researchers, Inc.; p. 7 Wendy Shattil/Oxford Scientific Films; p. 8 Wm. Grenfell/Visuals Unlimited; pp. 9L, 19, 20 Joe McDonald/Visuals Unlimited; p. 9R Gary W. Carter/Visuals Unlimited; p. 10 Visuals Unlimited; p. 11 Bill Ivy/Fraser Photos; p. 12 T C Nature/Oxford Scientific Films; p. 13 Dwight Kuhn; p. 14 Zig Leszczynski/Animals Animals; p. 15 Joe McDonald/DRK Photos; p. 16 C. K. Lorenz/Photo Researchers, Inc.; p. 17 Howie Garber; p. 18 Tom J. Ulrich/Visuals Unlimited; p. 21 Walt Anderson/Visuals Unlimited; p. 22 Anthony Merciega/Photo Researchers, Inc.

Cover photograph by Joe McDonald/Visuals Unlimited

Every effort has been made to contact copyright holders of any material reproduced in this book.
Any omissions will be rectified in subsequent printings if notice is given to the publisher.

Special thanks to our advisory panel for their help in the preparation of this book:

Eileen Day, Preschool Teacher
Chicago, IL

Ellen Dolmetsch,
Library Media Specialist
Wilmington, DE

Kathleen Gilbert,
Teacher
Round Rock, TX

Sandra Gilbert,
Library Media Specialist
Houston, TX

Angela Leeper,
Educational Consultant
North Carolina Department
of Public Instruction
Raleigh, NC

Pam McDonald, Reading Teacher
Winter Springs, FL

Melinda Murphy,
Library Media Specialist
Houston, TX

The publisher would also like to thank Dr. Dennis Radabaugh, Professor of Zoology at Ohio Wesleyan University in Delaware, Ohio, for his help in reviewing the contents of this book.

Some words are shown in bold, **like this.**
You can find them in the picture glossary on page 23.

Contents

What's Awake?

Some animals are awake when you go to sleep.

Animals that stay awake at night are **nocturnal**.

Skunks are awake at night.

What Are Skunks?

Skunks are **mammals**.

Mammals have **fur**.

Mammals live with their babies.

Mammals make milk for the babies.

What Do Skunks Look Like?

Skunks are black with white stripes down their backs.

They have bushy tails.

skunk

cat

Skunks are the size of cats.

Skunks have small eyes and ears.

9

Where Do Skunks Live?

In the wild, skunks live in forests and **grasslands**.

They sleep in **burrows** of other animals.

In the city, skunks live under porches or under buildings.

What Do Skunks Do at Night?

Skunks spend the night looking for food.

They can eat all night.

Sometimes skunks wake up late
in the afternoon.

Then, they come out of
their **burrows.**

What Do Skunks Eat?

In the wild, skunks eat small animals and bugs.

They eat fruit and leaves, too.

In the city, skunks eat these things, too.

They also eat garbage or food people leave out for their pets.

What Do Skunks Sound Like?

Skunks are usually quiet.

Sometimes they make a whistling noise.

Skunks can also make a
screeching noise.

They might screech when they
are mad or afraid.

How Are Skunks Special?

Skunks do not often fight.

Instead, they squirt a spray at their enemies.

The spray smells bad.

But skunks only spray when there is danger.

Where Do Skunks Go during the Day?

In the morning, skunks go back to their **burrows.**

They go to sleep.

They sleep until it begins to get dark again.

Skunk Map

fur   stripe   tail

Picture Glossary

burrow
pages 10, 13, 20

mammal
pages 6, 7

fur
page 6

nocturnal
page 4

grasslands
page 10

Note to Parents and Teachers

Reading for information is an important part of a child's literacy development. Learning begins with a question about something. Help children think of themselves as investigators and researchers by encouraging their questions about the world around them. In this book, the animal is identified as a mammal. A mammal by definition is one that is covered with hair or fur and that feeds its young with milk from its body. The symbol for mammal in the picture glossary is of a dog nursing its babies. Point out the fact that, although the photograph for mammal shows a dog, many other animals are mammals—including humans.

 CAUTION: Remind children that it is not a good idea to handle wild animals. Children should wash their hands with soap and water after they touch any animal.

Index